work that God sees

prayerful motherhood
in the midst of the overwhelm

----

growing

----

shannon guerra

Copyright © 2019 Shannon Guerra

All rights reserved. No part of this book may be reproduced in any form or by any electronic or mechanical means, including information storage and retrieval systems, without permission in writing from the publisher, except by reviewers, who may quote brief passages in a review.

ISBN 978-0-9600921-6-1
ISBN (ebook) 978-0-9600921-7-8

Scripture quotations are from the ESV® Bible (The Holy Bible, English Standard Version®), copyright © 2001 by Crossway, a publishing ministry of Good News Publishers. Used by permission. All rights reserved.

Portions of scripture in **bold** are the author's emphasis.

Cover design by Copperlight Wood

This title may be purchased in bulk for ministry or group study use. For more information, please email shop@copperlightwood.com.

Printed and bound in the United States of America

Published by Copperlight Wood
P.O. Box 870697
Wasilla, AK   99687

www.copperlightwood.com

for Robin,

who lives deep and wide

and knows how to press on

Also by Shannon Guerra

Upside Down:
Understanding and Supporting Attachment in Adoptive and Foster Families

Oh My Soul:
Encountering God in Honest, Unconventional (and Sometimes Messy) Prayer

Oh My Soul Companion Journal

Oh My Soul Devotional:
21-Day Complete Study
3-Day Mini Studies

the Work That God Sees series:
Prayerful Motherhood in the Midst of the Overwhelm
Capable
Allied
Growing
Steadfast
Resilient
Seen

growing:
a definition
7

an accidental feast:
how we rise when we think we've made a flop
9

the sweet school:
parenting wisdom from Titus 3
13

warmly, xoxo
and other things I've told you, yada yada
15

obiter dictum:
observations along the way
18

taking inventory
at the doorway of a New Year
19

A.W. Tozer:
on being prepared for whatever the New Year brings
24

just one lesson:
to be like You when I grow up
25

Jane Addams:
how great men make their mark upon history
33

what comes next:
going deep or going wide, and running with it
34

Charlotte Mason:
on becoming magnanimous
39

the party of deep & wide:
nurturing an atmosphere of growth
40

Madeleine L'Engle:
the need to make incarnate
46

thumbless mittens:
a pattern for knitters
47

felted thumbless mittens:
a more ambitious pattern for knitters
49

questions
for personal journaling or group discussion
53

notes
56

growing

growing:
adjective. advancing, maturing

see also:
forging ahead, going places, improving, increasing, learning, moving forward, on the march, pressing on

gaining ground

this is who you are.

an accidental feast

how we rise when
we think we've made a flop

He was almost ten years old. Afton was looking at the largest baking bowl we owned, full of flour and some other white ingredient, which, from the look on his face, was probably called "regret."

I asked him what it was. He said it was four cups of flour, and four teaspoons – or was it tablespoons? – of baking powder. Uh oh.

"What are you trying to make?"

He pointed to the cookbook. "Jalapeño cheese bread, but it's a double batch." And that sounded awesome, but he was using a cornbread recipe and he'd actually quadrupled it. I tried to explain that he had to switch recipes and make the cornbread instead, and it was okay, because I could help him figure out the ratios and such…but, no, he said. It was not okay. Panic was setting in, and he started speaking desperately, without punctuation:

"I needed four cups but I was using the half-cup scoop so I did eight scoops but I don't want any cornmeal and do I really have to make cornbread because I want it to be like French bread *but I don't want to have to wait for it to rise!*"

The rising thing always gets me, too. But no, I told him, you can't make French bread, cheesy or otherwise, with baking powder. It needs yeast; it has to rise.

There was a quiet, tense pause. Then he said:

"I think I can separate the flour from the baking powder with static electricity."

And this, my friends, is why people are afraid to homeschool. They *say* it's because they can't teach high school math, but the truth is they're terrified their nine-year-old is going to blow up the kitchen by separating flour from baking powder using static electricity.

(That night during dinner cleanup, we asked him where he heard about that. He shrugged and said it was from a science book. I turned to Vince and announced, "That does it. No more science.")

But four batches of cornbread later (perfect, cheesy, drool-worthy, jalapeño cornbread), he learned a lesson that we all get eventually: Things don't always work out the way we expect, and we don't always end up where we planned.

As I type this, we've lived in the Matanuska Valley for eleven years but never expected to end up in Wasilla. We initially resisted moving at all and justified it with reasons that sounded good on the surface, but it turned out that what we were staying for in Anchorage was exactly what God was trying to get us away from. He had something so much better for us, if we would trust Him enough to let go.

And we did let go. But we thought we were supposed to move just a little north of Anchorage to Eagle River, and when we started looking, there was nothing available there. We searched and prayed and eventually went with plan B: Even farther north, we found land in Palmer. We made plans and a million phone calls, hired subcontractors to build a house, and then ten days before we were supposed to break ground, our bank went under. So that didn't work out, either.

Sometimes when things don't work out, fear starts to take root: What if this is the beginning of a pattern, and the next bend in the road is even worse? What if we think He told us to do this, but we heard wrong? What if we're just waiting for the next shoe to drop?

But what if none of those scenarios are the case at all?

What if the things in our lives that aren't working out *only seem that way* because they're not finished yet?

What if we are judging the end product by the messy middle phase? Like cake or cornbread that needs to bake for an hour, but we pull it out of the oven when it's still doughy and unset – we followed the recipe, used all the right ingredients, but we checked its progress too early. It's not done yet because there's no shortcut to waiting for it to rise.

I still don't know why He didn't just tell us right out to move to Wasilla. Maybe He knew it was too far off our radar and we had to warm up to the idea, or maybe there were timing issues. Maybe He knew we were stubborn (pfft, whatever) and He wanted to test our obedience. Maybe it was a million different things.

Maybe He wanted to teach us that even when life doesn't go the way we plan, it still works out. He knew we would need to remember that in the years ahead.

The end product might not look at all like what we signed up for. It might not be what we wanted at all — no one plans ahead to anticipate disease, disaster, divorce, or other heartbreak. That's fair; He doesn't want those things either, and He grieves with us. But He is the master at taking the most screwed up recipes — all of our accidents, failures, and near-misses — and even when it feels like we're having nothing but hot water for dinner, He's redeeming it all into a gourmet feast.

Life needs yeast in order to rise.

And sometimes, things are hard simply because that's the nature of expanding our comfort zone, living and learning deep and wide. It's not because we are failing; it's because we are not those who shrink back...even from homeschool.

That same kid, a few days later, was right back at it — and this time he had a project he wanted to tackle with the sewing machine. The fabric was stretchy, the machine was unfamiliar, and he looked up at me.

"I prayed first," he said, and hit the pedal.

the sweet school
parenting wisdom from Titus 3

Just finished cutting duct tape out of an eight-year-old's hair. It must be my fault; I've been a mom for all these years and never thought to tell our kids that duct tape does not make effective noise-cancelling earmuffs.

There is a pile of laundry on the bench and another load rolling in the dryer, and that teething boy has already wiped his nose all over the sweater I'm wearing so the washer will be full again soon, too. Some of the kids are finishing school for the week. Others have refused lessons all week and chose instead to learn things the hard way for the umpteenth week in a row. But this is the sweet school, and I'm pretty sure I'm learning more than the kids.

I keep coming back to this, and it settles my focus in what we are doing as parents:

Remind them to be submissive to rulers and authorities,
to be obedient,
to be ready for every good work,
to speak evil of no one,
to avoid quarreling,

*to be gentle,
and to show perfect courtesy toward all people.
For we ourselves were once foolish, disobedient,
led astray...*

- Titus 3:1-3a

And I need to focus, because these guys can be fantastic little sinners sometimes, yes?

They're just like us, just like we were. And good gravy, if He can clean us up when we were such a mess, just think of what He can do with our kids.

warmly, xoxo
and other things I've told you, yada yada

The nativity and garland were both on the mantle, and many years' worth of accumulated paper snowflakes hung from the ceiling. The tree was up, with lights and ornaments and strands of popcorn clinging to it. Because we're nice parents, we let the kids decorate it. But because we also prefer not to have all the decorations clustered on the same three branches of the tree, we rearranged everything when they weren't looking.

And later, in spite of how many times we'd told her to be careful, when a crash came from that vicinity we found then-four-year-old Chamberlain staring in shock at the dangerous, glittery mess of shards before her.

"It bwoke!" she gasped. "*Oh!!* So it *is* bweakable!"

So, we were festive. We were merry. But also, we were freezing.

It was minus 22 outside so I didn't send the kids out to play; we made forts, paintings, and other messes inside, instead. The temperature doesn't really matter, because when it's cold outside we can still keep it warm inside. Unless we don't.

Unless there's bickering and bossing, snapping and strife, and I assign consequences and replay lectures all day long. The temperature drops in our connections, and it takes a lot of hugs, kisses, and happy conversations to warm things up again.

It was warmer the week before – outside, at least – and the kids were sledding and hollering on the hill behind us. And they knew (*they knew,* I tell you) about waiting to go down until the people at the bottom of the hill have moved out of the way so they don't slam into them. Especially if it's the littlest sister at the bottom of the hill. *Especially* if all five of her siblings are piled into one sled and bowling into her.

But no, there's screaming and bossing and sheepish giggling and fuming and praise God, no blood, but mine is boiling. *I have told you and told you...*yada, yada. I wiped her tears and gave severe looks to older children and sent them all off to play again.

Thirty seconds later, I peeked out the window to check on everyone. Two brothers were thrashing each other in the snowbank next to the sledding hill.

I knocked fiercely on the kitchen window to get their attention. Three kids turned to look, and in my aggressive charades I pointed to the eldest, who paused his friendly pummeling. I motioned "STOP" á la The Supremes, and he gave me a questioning look, as though he couldn't hear me.

I was about to holler "I *KNOW* YOU CAN *UNDERSTAND* ME" through the glass, but his little brother shoved him from behind, faceplanting him in the snow.

Fine, whatever.

A few minutes later they were back to sledding, going down the icy hill on their bellies, on their bottoms, on their boots. And after years of experience, this is a no-no, because sliding down rough, icy hills using expensive polyurethane thermal attire in lieu of sleds is terrible stewardship of snow gear. The preferred method of repair is not, I'm sorry to say, my superior sewing skills. It is duct tape, Alaska chic.

Every winter we take inventory to see what fits, what can be grown into, and what is beyond even the appreciable scope of duct tape and must be replaced.

And we've talked about it. A lot. *I have told you and told you*...blah, blah, blah.

They finally came in from sledding and I assigned chores to make up for the extra money we would have to spend on more snowpants if they kept using them as toboggans. While they warmed up over tea, we talked about patches instead of replacements.

I reminded the boys that we still had Iree's old snowpants – the ones that were duct-taped on the rear from the previous two years. They still had lots of usable material on them that could be used for patches. Nice, thick, padded...hot pink...material.

Perfect. Festive, and merry.

I informed the boys that it would be used on their snowpants, should patches become necessary. And just to remind them how much I love them – because *I had told them and told them*, but sometimes they just don't listen – I also threatened to practice my sewing skills, and embroider a little something on those patches as a reminder:

XOXO.

obiter dictum:

observations along the way

●●●●●●●●●●●●●●●●●●●●●●

It turns out that when you are craving chocolate, caramel, coconut, cinnamon something-or-other... eating a banana does NOT make you feel better.

●●●●●●●●●●●●●●●●●●●●●●

Dear family: The little stickers on fruits and veggies are not supposed to go in the compost, even if they DO say "organic." Sincerely, the Management

●●●●●●●●●●●●●●●●●●●●●●

Having a young child brush your hair is akin to luxurious spa treatment sporadically interrupted with ancient methods of torture.

●●●●●●●●●●●●●●●●●●●●●●

Attention Fred Meyer shoppers: The signs are a little mixed up in the pepper section today, so those little orange ones labeled "orange bell peppers" are, in fact, habeneros. Know your produce or pay the consequences.

●●●●●●●●●●●●●●●●●●●●●●

I've gotten my kids to be quiet just by whispering, "Shh! What is that?!" Then we all listened to the refrigerator humming for at least ten seconds. It was beautiful.

taking inventory
at the doorway of a New Year

By the end of December, after Christmas and on the edge of a New Year, it was back up to forty degrees. We looked out on a bleak day with fallen branches and rippling puddles and hurricane winds, because, Alaska.

We woke up to a power outage in the wee hours. All was darkness, and in the house there was a heavy quiet, but outside the wind and rain were hissing and rasping. Vince fumbled for his phone to check the time and we had a couple of hours before he had to leave for work. The wind had knocked the power out from Willow to Sutton – across most of the Matanuska Valley – and we could expect it to take a while to come back on. We took inventory in thoughts and whispers.

There are dirty dishes all over the kitchen counter. Shoot, my phone is only at 50%. I knew I should've filled the water glass in the bathroom last night. The teapot is probably empty, too. These are the things we think of.

"I can charge your phone in the car before I leave," Vin whispered. One thing fixed. But we were going to have to drag up water from the crawlspace, and we hadn't filled a fresh water jug in weeks. We strategized water and toiletry needs while trying not to wake up the kids and also trying not to feel like irresponsible parents and out of practice Alaskans.

I tried a different tack and started ticking off our assets. *The kids have all showered. The dishes in the dishwasher are clean. I have water by the bed. We did all the laundry yesterday. We have plenty of candles, and I set beans to soak last night. Hey, we're not doing that bad.*

The power came back on at our house before Vin had to leave, and he was able to make rice, store fresh water, make coffee, and fill a sink full of soapy water in case the power went out again while he was at work. We were ready if we needed to be.

That afternoon, our youngest daughter came to me with an old bag stuffed full of goodies over her shoulder. She stopped in front of me and pretended to knock on an invisible door between us.

"Open the door, Mom!"

I pretended to open the door, and Chamberlain bounced in giddy enthusiasm.

"I have presents for you!" she announced. "Guess what they are!"

We used to play this game all the time. "Is it...a baby doll? Is it...tiramisu? Is it...a nap?" *Dream on, Mama.*

"Nooo..." she giggled, grinning, swinging the bag. "It starts with Y," she whispered, trying to help.

"Oh! Is it...yarn? Is it...a yellow crayon?"

"No!! It's...an ALLIGATOR!"

Of course. A yalligator.

The New Year was upon us, and all sorts of things knocked at the door. Every year we make lists and goals and resolutions to do more, be more, read more, earn more, give more. We are ambitious and hopeful. But by the end of the year when we take inventory, we are always surprised – and maybe a little discouraged – by what we didn't accomplish.

Cham came back with an armload of stuffed animals, and knocked again on the invisible door between us.

"Open it, Mom!"

I did, and she started dispensing stuffed animals into my lap.

"Wait!" I told her. "You're supposed to tell me who you are and what you're bringing me. Are you from the zoo again? The bakery? Are you bringing food?"

She thought for a second and then assumed her squeakiest pretend voice.

"Hi. I'm Chamberwain Gewa, and -" she piled more buddies into my lap "- I left half of the babies at home because they're sick, but their daddy is with them and I hafta run to the store, so you need ta watch these ones for me until I get back."

"Oh. Am I...the grandma?"

She sighed. "Yes!!!" Obviously, this explains the lack of introduction when she knocked on my door. If I'd had a nap, I might've been a little quicker at figuring out this game.

We know – as you do, too – that not everything that knocks on the door of a new year announces itself with good manners or a sweet smile or even gives us time to prepare for its arrival. Some things knock on the door that we will simply refuse to answer, knowing that not everything a new year wants to dump in our laps is healthy for our family. Other things, worse than windstorms and power outages, barge their way in and give us no choice. But overall, we know – as I hope you do, too – that we can have great expectations for the coming year.

Every New Year's Day, Vince and I talk about our goals for the year – we look over our old goals list, evaluate how we're doing long-term, fudge the dates on things we want to put off for a while, and type out the new list for the new year.

Except one year. That year, for the first time, we didn't even pull out the goals list. I'm not sure why, probably it was partly due to a crazy schedule and we just kept pushing it aside, but it was more than that. It came down to feeling overrun – I didn't want any more obligations, whether I was making them for myself or not. Unmet goals feel like failure. And this parenting gig can be rough; we certainly don't need any more of that.

We can put such pressure on ourselves to meet ridiculous expectations. We have this terrible inclination to take inventory and think that our assets are woefully lacking. Our checklist of things we wanted to accomplish in a year comes short at the end of December and we realize there were so many things we meant to do that never happened.

And that's okay. If you are coming to the New Year in a hard season that looks far different from what you pictured twelve months ago, it does not mean that you failed. It means you made it. You are growing. We are growing. And we're in good company, because Jesus had to grow, too:

And the child grew and became strong, filled with wisdom. And the favor of God was upon him.

- Luke 2:40

By the end of the year, we can also be buoyed by the things we *did* achieve that we never realized were possibilities at the beginning of the year. And we can expect the New Year ahead to hold similar surprising opportunities, too.

Seek first the kingdom of God and His righteousness, and all these things will be added to you.

- Matthew 6:33

Our real goal is not to do more, be more, or earn more. It is to find Him more, to see Him more, to hear Him more.

He stands with us at the threshold of every day, shining the light in, asking the hardest questions in the gentlest manner. And everything else comes with Him. Maybe even a Yalligator...and a nap.

I do not advise that we end the year on a somber note. The march, not the dirge, has ever been the music of Christianity.

If we are good students in the school of life, there is much that the years have to teach us. But the Christian is more than a student, more than a philosopher. He is a believer, and the object of his faith makes the difference, the mighty difference.

Of all persons the Christian should be best prepared for whatever the New Year brings. He has dealt with life at its source. In Christ he has disposed of a thousand enemies that other men must face alone and unprepared. He can face his tomorrow cheerful and unafraid because yesterday he turned his feet into the ways of peace and today he lives in God.

The man who has made God his dwelling place will always have a safe habitation.

- A.W. Tozer[1]

just one lesson
to be like You when I grow up

Christmas brought new sleds, and the New Year brought four inches of fresh snow, and our yard was waiting to be violently trampled by our six kids who frantically donned snow gear and repeatedly slammed the garage door as they raced outside, each hauling a plastic disk that promised to hurtle them down the hill at warp speed.

Except for one kid, who was sobbing and wailing in depths of despair that would make Anne Shirley proud.

"*This mitten* won't fit on *this* hand! And *this* mitten is on *this* hand" – she thrust it at me as evidence – "but the OTHER mitten won't fit on my OTHER hand because ITS thumb is on THIS side!!"

She flung both her arms out to show me. "LOOK!" Her elementary vocabulary was limited, but what she really meant was, *Hey! This contrary mitten dares to defy me! Behold!*

I was beholding. The thumbs did look funny. The mitten also looked funny. She had it on the wrong hand, upside down.

I took that mitten off and held both of them in front of her so she could see what was wrong.

"This is how you had them," I said. "Now, watch this."

I flipped the mitten over and switched them to the correct hands, and they fit. No sticky-outy thumbs or anything, and all was right with the world.

She was little, and learning. But we all try to put things on in the wrong places, and then fly into despair when they don't fit right.

Moms especially learn that all of the discipline, training, and schooling that worked for their first kid usually won't be a perfect fit for the next child. Kids are designed with the irritating trait of resisting to mold perfectly to the likeness of others – they won't be made into their older siblings, and they won't be made into their parents. We may share many traits and features with our kids, but they were created to mold perfectly to the image of the One who made them...and He doesn't fit into any box we can come up with.

We have differing personalities and sometimes, we have short tempers. We have special needs and often incompetent, pat answers. We are kept on our toes and on our knees.

> *Consider it pure joy, my brothers and sisters, whenever you face trials of many kinds, because you know that the testing of your faith produces perseverance. Let perseverance finish its work so that you may be mature and complete, not lacking anything.*
>
> *-James 1:2-4*

Some days we are all thumbs, and they're sticking out in the wrong directions all over the place: *This kid* won't respond to *this consequence* and *this teaching style* doesn't work for *this kid* and we are stretched and grown beyond our parenting wisdom, and we cry for more.

If any of you lacks wisdom, you should ask God, who gives generously to all without finding fault, and it will be given to you.

- James 1:5

Honestly, what we're really saying is, *Hey! These contrary children dare to defy me! Behold!* We thrust the situation and these children and all of the sore thumbs at Him, and He gently shows us how to put things upright again. He shows us how He made us all to fit together.

Instead, we will speak the truth in love, growing in every way more and more like Christ, who is the head of his body, the church. He makes the whole body fit together perfectly. As each part does its own special work, it helps the other parts grow, so that the whole body is healthy and growing and full of love.

- Ephesians 4:15-16

As we pray for wisdom, for our kids and all of our differences, He does more than just show us how He is making our kids into His image. He makes us more into His image, too.

At dinnertime, the chili simmered on the stove, the cheese was shredded in a bowl, and a plate of crackers was set out and ready. Only the onions were left, and I diced those up, wiping my watery eyes, and shooed a kid away from the counter.

I gotta tell you, nowadays that kid does most of the cooking. But when he was five he was always in the kitchen, in the middle of the action, and sometimes, yes, a little in the way.

"Don't get too close or you'll learn a lesson," I warned him. "These onions are fierce." I sniffled and blinked away tears.

He grinned at me. He was a red-haired thrill-seeker who couldn't pronounce his L's yet, undaunted and disbelieving.

"Aww, no way...can I smell 'em? I want to wearn a wesson!"

Sure. This will be fun.

I set down the knife and gestured toward the pile of onions. He leaned forward and took a huge, reckless whiff.

"See?" he said, blinking. "It doesn't...*aaahhh*!!" Oh, experience...that most thorough of teachers. He wearned his wesson, alright.

There are so many lessons every day, and not all of them come with such entertainment. We're often overwhelmed with a mental checklist of what we must teach our children, because we're still learning, too. And if we could just get them to flush the toilet on a regular basis, we might have confidence in our ability to teach them the other important stuff.

The task of education seems staggering. Whether we homeschool, private school, public school, or preschool, it's ultimately our job to prepare our kids for life after they leave the nest.

Take a deep breath, mama. Group hug. I have good news for both of us.

We can get overwhelmed and muddled with all of the details, but the real objective is simple. When we filter out the distractions and distill the broadness of "education" down to its purest purpose, we find that our focus is clear.

We teach our kids a million little lessons every day so they will know just one thing: We want them to know Jesus. Everything comes down to this.

We want them to explore the world He created so they will understand the immensity of its Creator. We want them to learn about the people who live here so they will understand His heart for those He loves. And we want them to know Him so much that they become more like Him – loving and truthful, wise and good, reflecting the Father who loves them.

And that covers every subject. When we teach these small humans, it's more than filling them with information. We are building up a person, a family, a generation, and a kingdom.

I mean, no pressure or anything. Need some smelling salts? Another hug?

There's more good news, though: We don't have to know everything or be an expert on every subject. We are teachable, too - learning alongside them and making mistakes with them, saved from the pressure and façade of perfection.

One day our oldest son headed out to the garage to do chores when my daughter asked, "Mom, is Jupiter made from gas like Saturn, or is it a normal planet?"

Ooh. This is not my area of expertise. I'm still confused about the whole Pluto controversy, and at that moment my planetary whiz had just left the room.

The garage door slammed as I answered, "I'm not sure...ask your brother. He would know."

The next instant, the garage door reopened, and my son yelled, "Yep! Jupiter's made from gas!" and the door slammed again. She had her answer, and I was off the hook.

We are always learning, all of us.

For this very reason, make every effort to supplement your faith with virtue, and virtue with knowledge, and knowledge with self-control, and self-control with steadfastness, and steadfastness with godliness, and godliness with brotherly affection, and brotherly affection with love. For if these qualities are yours and are increasing, they keep you from being ineffective or unfruitful in the knowledge of our Lord Jesus Christ.

- 2 Peter 1:5-8

When we are teachable, our kids learn they can trust us. If a person is humble enough to grow, lean into God, admit mistakes, and tackle unfamiliar territory, they can probably be trusted with issues of the heart, too. Not every lesson in life is simple, and when our kids encounter gritty situations or deep questions, they need thoughtful answers from a heart they can trust.

The way we learn alongside them and in front of them, influences their future mightily. They learn by watching and imitating us, putting their own spin on things as they navigate new experiences.

In those days, our youngest daughter had claimed a new baby doll, but it wasn't what you'd expect. Nope, friends, her new baby was a small vacuum named Little Guy – not to be confused with our regular vacuum that the kids called Big Guy, or with Super Guy, the steam cleaner, of course.

She brought me the vacuum, awkwardly cradled in her arms and weighing almost as much as she did. "Mom, can you change Little Guy's diaper?"

It was late afternoon and I was finally eating lunch, so I shook my head.

She sighed – where did she learn *that*? - and mumbled, "He's got a stinky, poopy diaper *again*. I keep changing his stinky diapers" – she heaved Little Guy over her shoulder with another sigh – "and he just keeps *making* them. Come on, let's go change you..."

This sounds eerily familiar, but I promise you I've never changed a vacuum's diaper before.

She finished a few minutes later (the poor dishtowel she used was never the same) and she approached the couch where her brother was sitting.

"Can you move? My baby needs to take a nap." Her brother kindly refused and indicated the window seat as an alternative, where she gently put down her charge and covered it with a blanket.

For better or worse, seeds of our own behavior are brought to accountability when we see them sprout and manifest in our children. If we sigh, they learn to sigh. If we complain, they learn to complain. If we are tender and gentle, they befriend the vacuum that nobody likes.

We cultivate these little arrows in our quiver until they are grown and ready to fly out into the world. We want them to know that when we are like Jesus, it somehow also makes us more unique, more informed and prepared for the future, and more wildly individual than we could ever imagine ourselves to be.

We teach them over and over, every day, in a million ways, so they will know this. So they will be like Him when they grow up.

And if your kids are like my kids, they'll probably ask you a certain, burning question about this.

Did Jesus have to pick up His Legos, too?

Yes, dear, He sure did. I'm afraid so.

Our kids will rattle around in our three-bedroom, two-bath quiver for eighteen years or so. In that time, we prepare them to be launched from that harp with one string, striking a chord for the kingdom.

Each of these kids, full and blooming with their gifts and abilities and passions, are a single individual note just bursting with their exclusive, unique tone, brought into harmony with all of the other notes at play.

Your kids. My kids. Their kids. All destined to make a song that will impact the nations with its music, long after they leave the nest, long after we leave this earth.

And I will make every effort so that after my departure you may be able at any time to recall these things.

- 2 Peter 1:15

We teach them the music for their joy, for His glory, and for the Kingdom's growth, in perfect time. Every lesson we teach them comes down to how they play that one note.

Just that one. No one else will play it like they do.

What is a great man who has made
his mark upon history?

Every time, if we think far enough, he is a man
who has looked through the confusion of the moment
and has seen the moral issue involved;
he is a man who has refused to have his sense
of justice distorted; he has listened to his conscience
until conscience becomes a trumpet call to like-
minded men, so that they gather about him and
together, with mutual purpose and mutual aid,
they make a new period in history....

[T]he lessons of great men are lost unless
they re-enforce upon our minds the highest demands
which we make upon ourselves;
they are lost unless they drive our sluggish wills
forward in the direction of their highest ideals.

- Jane Addams [2]

what comes next

going deep or going wide, and running with it

Fair warning to our paleo, celiac, and other gluten-free friends: You might want to just skip this chapter. Or push through and take your chances, but don't say I didn't warn you.

You know those gifts you buy for your kids, but they're really sort of for you, too? Last Christmas we gave Iree and Afton a baking book (disclaimered with the wrapping paper that says "I bought this so we could share") because, well, they like to bake, but I really wanted to read it. So we gave it to them and they opened it, yawned, and moved onto more exciting presents while I curled up on the couch with the book and got to read the first few chapters in one sitting, which was my brilliant plan all along.

But a few days later they came around to it, and Afton in particular started taking a serious interest. He went beyond reading the narrative and dug into the recipes, which mentioned terms I'd never heard of before and also required a two or three day process to complete – which, as a quick-and-dirty baker myself, I'd also never heard of.

He was unintimidated. With only flour, salt, yeast, water, curious determination, and occasionally eggs, over one month he learned how to make sourdough and brioche, pane Genzano and pane de mie, and finally, baguettes. On that day, our homeschool supplementary material was brought to us by King Arthur Flour and their "How to Shape a Baguette" video.

I didn't realize a video was needed for this, but according to them you have to do some particular folding, and after that it's pretty much just like play dough: You roll out your dough like a snake until the skinny loaf is approximately the length of a sofa, and then, *viola!* Baguette.

Afton asked if I mind that he's cooking so much. (*Mind?* Eating fresh bread every day? I think I can suffer through it, I told him.) He asked if it was too expensive to keep baking and trying new recipes. We talked about the price of ingredients versus the price of bread in stores – cheap loaves, and the good stuff – and we looked up the bakery retail prices for the types of bread he's learning to make. We discovered that if the kid ever decides to go into business, he might be able to buy a small house in cash by the time he graduates high school.

So, no, this fascination with bread and baking is not costing us a thing.

And I almost dreaded telling him this lest it break the magic, but no, he's in deep, beyond the threat of a thin bubble bursting. So I told him that *what he's really doing is school, the way it's meant to be done* – finding that subject you love, and running with it.

Which leads me to a question, and I'm asking it of myself, too: Have you found a subject you love, and are you running with it?

And if not, before you beat yourself up by answering, *No, I wish I could, but we're hip-deep in (fill in the blank) and there's just no time,* let me suggest that you are growing in an entirely different way.

We have seasons when we we're too busy putting out fires to have time to light our own. Sometimes they are dark, or difficult, and last a really long time. Sometimes they are the season when we see no light at the end of the tunnel and we have no idea when, if, or how we will get through it. And if you are in that season, it sounds like a cruel joke to have more pressure put on you to find something you love and just run with it, because what you really need is oxygen, and space to breathe.

I want to tell you, friend, that you are growing, too. You are doing the hard work of character growth that we don't get to choose, but have to go through anyway. We might as well grow through it as we go through it.

Not everyone does, of course. Plenty of people are out there stagnating, just turning bitter and hopeless – I've been there, too – but my guess is that if you're still reading this, that's not you.

For me as I type this, it's a weird season because we're in the middle of both kinds of growth, and I'm not sure I've ever seen them so distinctly before: Finding the thing we love and running with it, but also being hip-deep in other things and feeling strong-armed into the hard work of character growth so the Lord can move us to the next level. Because that's what character growth is, of course – preparation for what comes next.

It reminds me of when I was in fourth grade. My teacher came to me with a graded assignment and said something to the effect of, *Shannon, this work is so good that I've entered you into this program where you can be published in [some cheaply bound school publication] and all you need to do is this other writing assignment. Congratulations, great job!*

An extra assignment, just for me. That no one else had to do. *Oh goody*. File that one under "No good deed goes unpunished." Duly noted.

But it's where we're at when He sees something in us that He wants to grow, and we go back to do more of the same work, hitting those hard foundations of confession, repentance, and prayer. These are the things we must go deep in, and keep returning to. We can never think we've graduated from the basics.

Search me, O God, and know my heart!
  Try me and know my thoughts!
And see if there be any grievous way in me,
  and lead me in the way everlasting!

- Psalm 139:23-24

We have to deal with the things deep inside before we can reach wide and expand our influence outside.

But, to go back to that extra writing assignment – you can see I might still need to process this – I've hesitated to assign many writing projects to my kids. I'm not sure how other writers who homeschool their children do it, but aside from journaling and narrations, we've preferred to let them write for fun (which they do) rather than give them a hate-of-learning experience with too many lengthy assignments, causing them to hate writing before they get a fair shot at falling in love with it. Too many of us were inoculated from the joy of learning by being force-fed an excessive assignment schedule, and it weakened our education instead of augmenting it.

So now, enter high school. Even though the dreaded five-paragraph essay is obsolete (and there was much rejoicing), our kids still need to know how to write.

And if learning to think hard and critically is one of the goals of education – and it is in this house – there's no better way to knuckle down and examine those thoughts than by doing the hard work of getting a required number of words on paper.

So Iree is going through a creative writing book and doing 500-word assignments, finding ideas and creativity simmering underneath that she had no idea existed, and the pieces emerging from her work are so good that I suspect she has possibly forgiven me for making her do it. Jury's still out though; I'd rather stick to my wishful thinking than ask her point-blank and have my hopes dashed with a negative answer.

Halfway through her book, it shifts from writing fiction to writing poetry. And because I am (sort of) a cool mom, I gave her the choice of finishing the book and doing the section on poetry, or skipping it and moving up to the next level of fiction assignments. She had weeks to think about it, and finally approached me to give me her answer in a roundabout fashion.

"I figured it out," she said. "I had to choose between deep and wide."

And my heart nearly exploded with the joy of a parent watching a child experience that eureka-moment of purpose. *Yes, Child, this is what education is about: Going deep, and going wide. It has always been thus.*

"I chose wide," she said. So, poetry it is. Time will tell if she decides to go deep and run with it.

Upon the knowledge of these great matters
- History, Literature, Nature, Science, Art -
the Mind feeds and grows.

It assimilates such knowledge
as the body assimilates food,
and the person becomes what is called
magnanimous,
that is,
a person of great mind,
wide interests,
incapable of occupying himself much
about petty, personal matters.

- Charlotte Mason[3]

the party of deep & wide
nurturing an atmosphere of growth

My husband is the one who first encouraged me to start think about public speaking. He said, in essence, You are a writer, and writers speak. And I shot back, No, I'm a writer, and writers write. Which sounded logical, but then a friend – and then another friend -- also brought it up.

And then, as He will do with Big Scary Things He Calls Us To, the Lord started bringing up the subject, and He is much harder to write off. I don't recommend it.

As though the Lord said, *I'll make you a deal you can't refuse*, a 20-week class on public speaking was offered at our church. And not just that, but it was free, it was with friends, and it was taught by another friend who knew what he was doing. The only catch was that it was scheduled for early in the morning, during those single-digit hours I prefer sleeping through. Why would I put myself through that?

I almost didn't. Too much work, too many things already going on, way the heck too early. I wasn't sure I could operate a blinker at that time of day, much less speak coherently in front of people.

But I knew I needed to. And when I argued with God about waiting until next year when the class would (maybe) be offered again, He shot back, *Hey Love, do you want to wait until next year for breakthrough, too?* Oh yes, He did. So I stopped whining about it and signed up.

It's something He told me to grow in, and growth is what we're called to.

So friends, here's what I learned:

The key to overcoming a fear of public speaking is to do it early in the morning, before you're lucid enough to know you shouldn't be standing in front of a bunch of people. Inhibitions are pretty low when you're semi-conscious.

It's a crazy vulnerable thing, though, standing in front of people, giving them your voice and your content, and offering your perspective. It's similar to writing but different in its aloud-ness – our very presence, standing in front of others, hoping they will be kind and gentle as we try not to make an idiot of ourselves.

But it was a safe place. The people in there with me were old friends and new friends, and we all needed encouragement, feedback, and grace. We weren't competing; we all wanted to do this better. Because none of us wants to look like an idiot when the time comes to be vulnerable.

We often have similar feelings and make similar efforts with other vulnerable areas of life, like social media, our relationship with people, our attendance in church, our efforts toward some Big Thing, or even our approach to Jesus. And we tend to do the same thing in those situations: We clean up a little, first. Just enough to look better than we are at the moment when inspiration strikes.

I should take that picture and post it on Instagram...but I'll straighten up the couch first.

I want to invite those people over to dinner...but first, I need to rearrange the living room.

I want to write a book, but first I should brush up on grammar and spelling.

I should go to church next Sunday...but I should try to stop swearing by Friday, first.

I'd love to reach out to that group...but they are more fill-in-the-blank (spiritual, educated, attractive, funny, gifted, whatever) than I am, so I want to be a little more fill-in-the-blank, too, first.

So I can fit in. So I don't disappoint. So I'm good enough.

The internet is loaded with trendy articles about how ridiculous our culture is, haranguing the insincerity of a superficial society that merely puts up a good front. And to some degree, they're right. Some of it is ridiculous.

But, you know what else? It's normal. And...it's also moderately healthy.

Record scratch. Yep, I heard it, too.

Hear me out. Insecurity and inflated egos are not healthy. But the desire to grow, to be better than we currently are, and to pursue improvement is healthy and good. If our efforts are sincere and genuine, and not simply a façade to impress others, we are on the right track.

Do we only clean our house for our Instagram photos, or are we genuinely trying to be a better keeper of our home, and this is part of our efforts?

Do we recognize we should behave better on a day-to-day basis, or are we just putting on a show around certain people?

Are we trying to prepare for a big new step, or are we just putting it off?

Are we inspired by others, or just trying to impress them?

Are we compelled toward greater things by our friends, or are we just competing with them?

The articles and media try to fit us into one of two opposing camps: the unpretentious hot messes versus the polished have-it-all-together types. But none of us are that black and white; we all excel in certain areas while faltering in others.

All of us are pushing through challenges and learning. So I propose we draw a new party line.

We are the party of deep and wide: Growing. Leaning further in our giftings, and stretching into unfamiliar territory. Looking at ourselves with a holy discontent, grateful for our progress but not satisfied with the status quo. Humble, genuine, imperfect, and refining daily.

This is the camp most of us actually fit in. The media can try to pit us into factions against each other, but we don't have to step into the ring. We're too aware of our own growth to point fingers at the lady who has spit up on her pants – or to raise an eyebrow at the lady who ironed perfect creases into hers.

We've heard that Jesus loves us as we are but He's not content to leave us there. Our own desire to do more, be more, know more, grow more, is something we've inherited from Him. It's what He wants for us, too.

So we fumble our way through, hoping those who see us will be kind and gentle as we try not to make an idiot of ourselves, because there is so much to learn.

The real human division is this: the luminous and the shady. To diminish the number of the shady, to augment the number of the luminous – that is the object. That is why we cry: Education! Science! To teach reading, means to light the fire; every syllable spelled out sparkles.

– Victor Hugo [4]

Let's be the people who cheer the efforts of others instead of projecting our insecurities onto them.

Show us the amazing meal you cooked, and tell us how it took you four times before you managed to get the cornstarch to thicken correctly. Tell us how great your kids are, and also the ridiculous way you had to remind them not to suck their underwear up the vacuum hose. Give us your church notes with messy handwriting, your gorgeous living room with imperfect furniture, your efforts at reading classic lit and your struggle to follow the intricate plot.

Show me your artwork, your craftsmanship, the amazing new technique you've been trying to perfect. No shame, no apologies to the peanut gallery. No internet lectures for showing off because you're more gifted in this one area than most of us.

I want to see that project you nailed, and how you killed it at your last performance. **I want to see your victories because they kindle more of mine.**

It's only our insecurity blending with resentment and jealousy that keeps us from cheering others on. That insecurity expresses itself in the disdain of judgement, just as it inhibits us from growing more in our own deep and wide.

On a bad day when my own struggle boils to the top, frustrated beyond sanity at fighting special needs, hard behaviors, and broken pasts, I admit I probably won't want to see your child's perfect certificate of achievement when one of mine spent the morning feigning confusion between the letters L and J (and he is confused, but not about the letters). But I promise the madness will pass and I'll be in my right mind again shortly, soon enough to praise your victory. Because when we're not in competition with each other, it's my victory, too.

Rather, speaking the truth in love, we are to grow up in every way into him who is the head, into Christ, from whom the whole body, joined and held together by every joint with which it is equipped, **when each part is working properly, makes the body grow so that it builds itself up in love.**

– *Ephesians 4:15-16*

We can be genuine while still inspiring each other to press on and be greater as we grow through this together.

So post your mess-in-progress. Don't apologize for where you've pulled it together. Show us where you're still stumbling, trying and fumbling, stretching out in your deep and your wide. Because we're called to growth, and this is your party.

A great painting, or symphony, or play,
doesn't diminish us, but enlarges us, and we, too,
want to make our own cry of affirmation
to the power of creation behind the universe.

This surge of creativity has nothing to do
with competition, or degree of talent.
When I hear a superb pianist, I can't wait to get
to my own piano, and I play about as well now as
I did when I was ten. A great novel, rather than
discouraging me, simply makes me want to write.

This response on the part of any artist
is the need to make incarnate
the new awareness we have been granted
through the genius of someone else.

- Madeleine L'Engle [5]

thumbless mittens
a pattern for knitters

Did you see that? These, my friends, are *thumbless* mittens for babies and toddlers. No right hand, no wrong hand. Life is complicated enough. You can see pictures of these mittens on my website here:
www.copperlightwood.com/wtgs-mittens

Materials:
1 skein of bulky superwash (washable) wool
1 set of 4 size 10.5 dpns (I prefer to use only three needles for this pattern, but you do what you want.)

Sizes: 0-12m (12-24m)

Gauge: 3.5 sts = 1" in the round

Abbreviations:
CO = cast on
BO = bind off
K = knit
St(s) = stitch(es)
K2tog = knit two stitches together
St st = stockinette stitch
Dpns = double-point needles

Directions:
CO 12 (16) sts and distribute sts among 3 needles. Knit in 1x1 rib (k1, p1) for 8 (12) rounds.

Increase as follows:
K 3 (4), pick up one st to end of round = 16 (20) sts.

Knit in St st for 9 (11) more rounds.

Decrease as follows:
Round 1: *K2 (3), k2tog* to end = 12 (16) sts.
Round 2: Knit even.
Round 3: *K1 (2), k2tog* to end = 8 (12) sts.
Round 4: Knit even.
Round 5: *K0 (1), k2tog* to end = 4 (8) sts.

For 0-12m size, pull yarn through loops and tie off.
For larger size, finish as follows:
Round 6: Knit even.
Round 7: *K0, k2tog* to end = 4 sts. Pull yarn through loops and tie off. Hide the ends and you're done!

...Unless you want to create a cord attachment to keep the mittens together, so as to not lose mittens every 2.5 times they play outside. To do so, measure your child's wingspan and knit an i-cord or crochet a tight chain of that length. Attach an end of this cord/chain to each of the mittens, and thread the whole shebang through their sleeves. If your cord/chain stretches out in an unwieldy manner, tie a knot in the middle of it (which will be hidden in the back of their jacket) to shorten it to the right size.

felted thumbless mittens

a more ambitious pattern for knitters

This is a complicated pattern, I admit.

I sold these for years through my knitting business and we still have several pairs; they are amazing in snowy weather as long as they don't get saturated. Wool is water-repellant – snow just balls up and sticks to it – so unless these mittens are submerged in a puddle or the snow has opportunity to repeatedly melt on them (like when children repeatedly come inside...) they will keep little hands warm, dry, and toasty.

You can see pictures of these mittens (including the tricksy cuff) on my website here:
www.copperlightwood.com/wtgs-mittens

Materials:
1 skein of worsted wool, or other "felt-able" fiber
1 set of 4 size 11 dpns
1 set of size 6 dpns

Sizes: 0-12m (12-24m, 2T-4T)

Gauge: 4 sts = 1" in the round

Abbreviations:
CO = cast on
BO = bind off
K = knit
St(s) = stitch(es)
K2tog = knit two stitches together
St st = stockinette stitch
Dpns = double-point needles

Directions:
CO 20 (24, 28) sts and distribute sts among 3 needles. Knit in St st for 20 (24, 28) rounds.

Decrease as follows:
Row 1: *K3 (4, 5), k2tog* to end = 16 (20, 24) sts.
Row 2: Knit even.
Row 3: *K2 (3, 4), k2tog* to end = 12 (16, 20) sts.
Row 4: Knit even.
Row 5: *K1 (2, 3), k2tog* to end = 8 (12,16) sts.
Row 6: Knit even.
Row 7: *K0 (1, 2), k2tog* to end = 4 (8, 16)sts. For 0-12m size, pull yarn through loops and tie off.
For larger sizes:
Row 8: Knit even.
Row 9: *K0(1), k2tog* to end = 4 (8) sts. For 12-24m size, pull yarn through loops and tie off.
Row 10: Knit even.
Row 11: *k2tog* to end = 4 sts. Pull yarn through loops and tie off.

These will look way too large and floppy, and that's okay. Trust me and repeat the process for the second mitten.

Weave in ends and felt; allow to dry overnight.

Wait!! What if I don't know how to felt?!

Don't worry, felting is easy. You know that time your husband did the laundry and ruined your favorite wool sweater because it shrunk up to nothing in the washing process? No, just me? Well, anyway, that is felting.

Wool fibers have tiny scales all over them that overlap and cling to each other, creating a thick, dense fabric when agitated. So throw the mittens in a sink half-filled with warm, sudsy water, and scrubscrubscrub them until they feel stiff (ish) and have shrunk to the size you need. Or do what I used to do, and find an enthusiastic kid to do it.

Okay, they're felted and dry. Now what?

Add the inner cuff: Fold the edge of the mitten cuff over about 1 inch (1 ½ -2 cm). Switch to size 6 dpns. Using the tip of one needle, attach yarn to the folded edge of the mitten by piercing through the felted stitches of the fabric and tying a knot. Then pierce through it again and pick up one stitch. Continue picking up and knitting 20 (24, 28) sts and distribute the stitches on your dpns.

Work a 1x1 rib (k1,p1) for 1 inch in the round (about 6 or 7 rounds).

BO *very loosely*, leaving 2 sts on needle; use these 2 sts to make an I-cord for about 4-5 inches. Sew in ends. Unfold outer cuff. Tada! You have felted mittens with an inner cuff, and a tie for tying the mittens together when they're not in use. When in use, the tie goes inside the mitten with the little chubby hand.

To care for finished mittens:

Do not, I repeat, do not throw these in the washer. They will felt even more (including the non-felted cuff you worked so hard to make) and shrink up beyond use.

Instead, gently wash by hand in cool water, careful not to agitate the fibers too much, and lay them out to dry. Or, just rinse them under the faucet in cool water, tie them together, and hang them over the faucet to drip dry into the sink.

questions
for personal journaling or group discussion

an accidental feast:

In your life right now, what is not working out the way you expected?

Are there any expectations or elements of control that I need to let go of, and surrender to God?

When I look back, what kind of "yeast" in my life has helped me rise? What did I learn in those situations?

the sweet school

What am I learning lately as I teach and discipline the kids?

Looking at each phrase of Titus 3:1-2, how am I currently living this out and modeling it for my kids?

As I pray about it, are there other ways I'd like to incorporate the elements of this passage into our home?

taking inventory

Looking at the past twelve months, what opportunities came that I never expected? What things did I accomplish that I didn't plan on?

What can I look forward to in the coming year?

What specific things do I hope to accomplish over the next twelve months? How can I break those things down into monthly or bi-weekly goals?

just one lesson

How am I modeling teachability and humility to my kids?

How am I learning in front of them and alongside them?

How do I see God making me more like Him in this season?

what comes next

Have I found a subject I love, and am I running with it? Or am I in a different kind of season, and growing in other ways?

When I look at my life right now, how is God preparing me for what comes next?

How can I go deeper in the foundations of confession, repentance, and prayer?

the party of deep & wide

What Big Thing(s) has the Lord been calling me to? What are my reasons, fears, or excuses for not doing it yet? What breakthrough in my life might be waiting for my obedience in this?

Where in my life do I have a holy discontent – where I'm grateful for my progress, but not satisfied with the status quo? What am I doing about it?

A checklist straight from the chapter – consider the questions that apply:

- Do I only clean our house for social media photos, or am I genuinely trying to be a better keeper of our home, and this is part of my efforts?
- Do I recognize I should behave better on a day-to-day basis, or am I just putting on a show around certain people?
- Am I trying to prepare for a big new step, or am I just putting it off?
- Am I inspired by others, or just trying to impress them?
- Am I compelled toward greater things by my friends, or am I just competing with them?

notes

1. A.W. Tozer, *The Warfare of the Spirit* (Chicago: Moody Publishers, 2006), 125, Scribd.

2. Jane Addams, "Address in Honor of George Washington on His Birthday," Speech. Chicago, IL, February 23, 1903.

3. Charlotte Mason, *Ourselves* (Quarryville, Penn: Charlotte Mason Research and Supply, 1989), 78.

4. Victor Hugo, *Les Miserables* (New York: Fall River Press, 2012), 614.

5. Madeleine L'Engle, *A Circle of Quiet* (San Francisco: HarperCollins, 1972), 147.

Also by Shannon Guerra

"What makes this book stand out from other contemporary Christian writings on prayer is the author's crisp prose and sharp sense of humor... An insightful, honest, and genuinely funny author delivers a standout devotional."

- *Kirkus Reviews*

It's significant that paper is made from the same material He was nailed to. He still uses it to heal us, show us more of Him, and conquer what's harassing us.

Available wherever books are sold, and at **copperlightwood.com**

Adoptive and foster families often feel alone, but it doesn't have to be that way. Shannon Guerra learned this first-hand after she and her husband adopted two children in 2012, and she started writing shockingly transparent blog posts about what her family was going through at home, at the doctor's office, and in her heart as a mama.

And adoptive and foster families started writing back. Their overwhelming, unanimous theme was, "This is what I've wanted to tell people for so long. **I wish everyone who knows our family could read this."**

Upside Down is the result. Because adoptive & foster families should never feel alone, & communities can be equipped to make sure they never feel that way again.

one more thing...

Do you want more encouragement in the season you're in? Do you want to grow deep and wide, regardless of your space and circumstances?

You are warmly invited to copperlightwood.com where we're transparent about finding peace in the hard moments, beauty in the mess, and white space in the chaos. It's a little unpolished here, so watch out for the Legos on the floor.

His peace is for you,

Shannon Guerra

subscribe:
eepurl.com/MugpP

connect:
instagram.com/copperlightwood
facebook.com/copperlightwood
goodreads.com/shannonguerra

www.ingramcontent.com/pod-product-compliance
Lightning Source LLC
Chambersburg PA
CBHW020628300426
44112CB00010B/1235